At the Beach

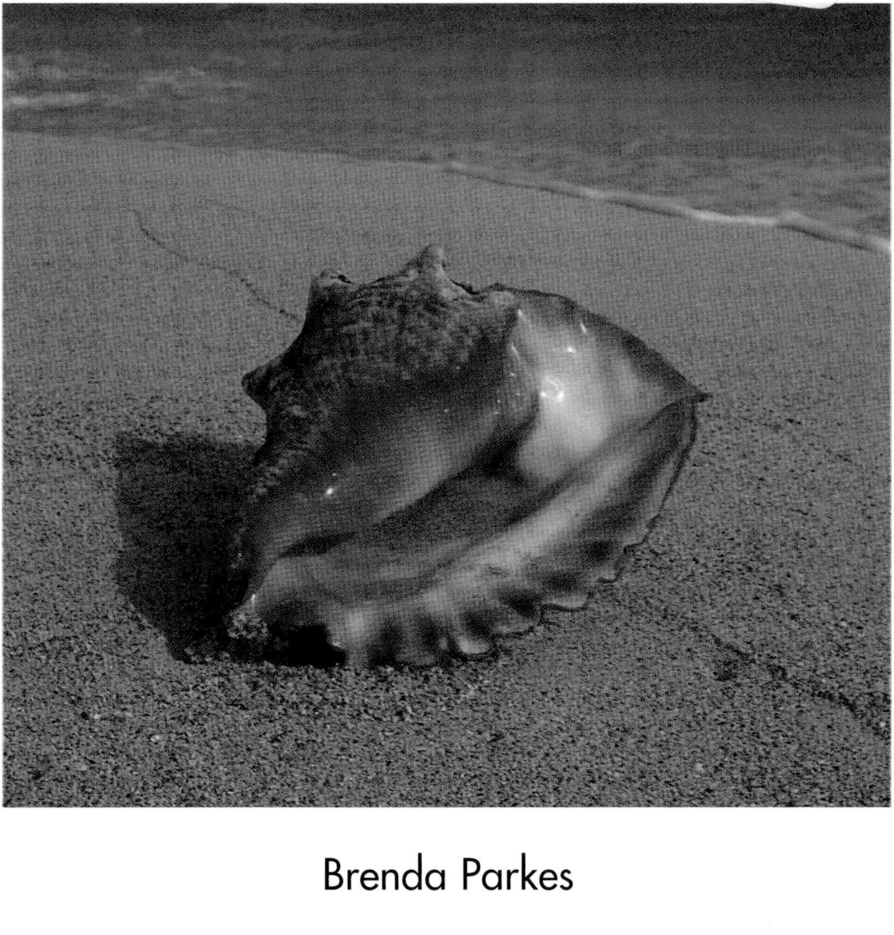

Brenda Parkes

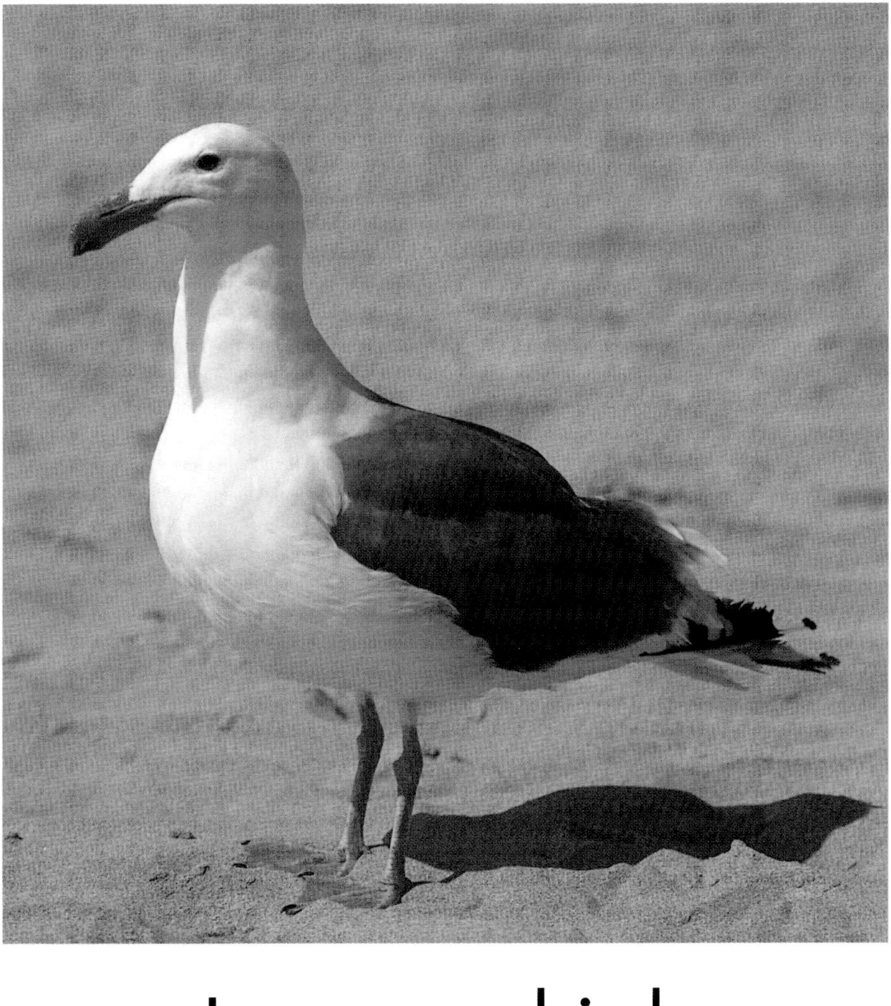

I saw a bird.

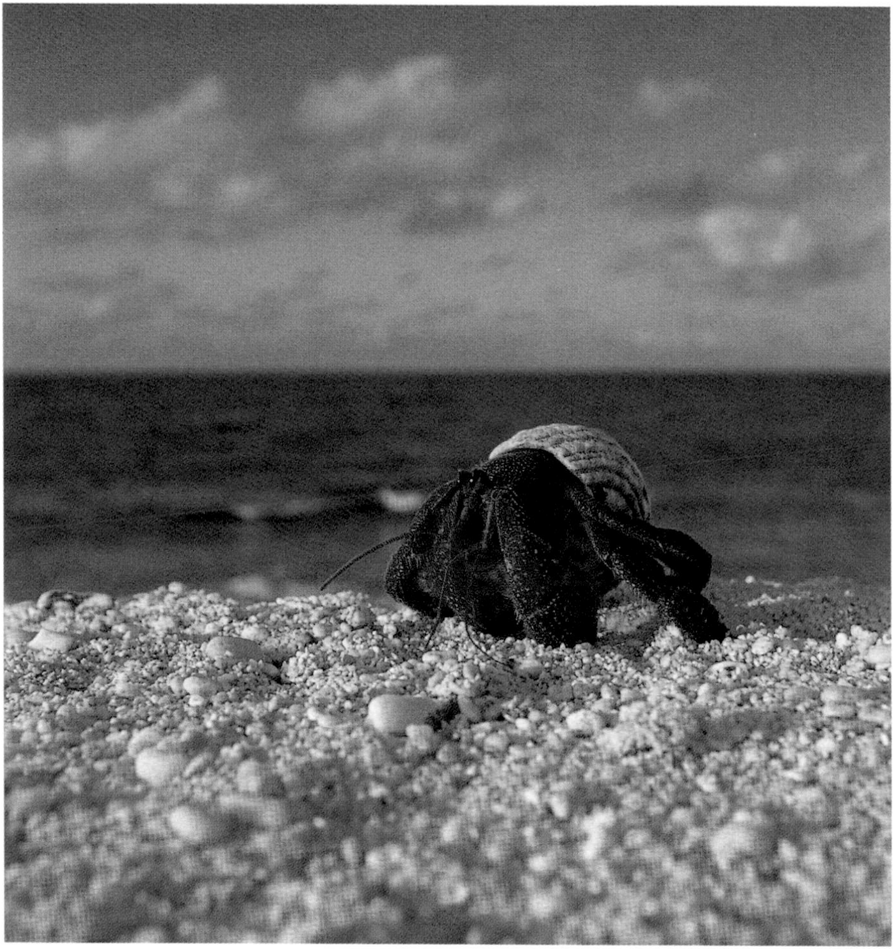

I saw a crab.

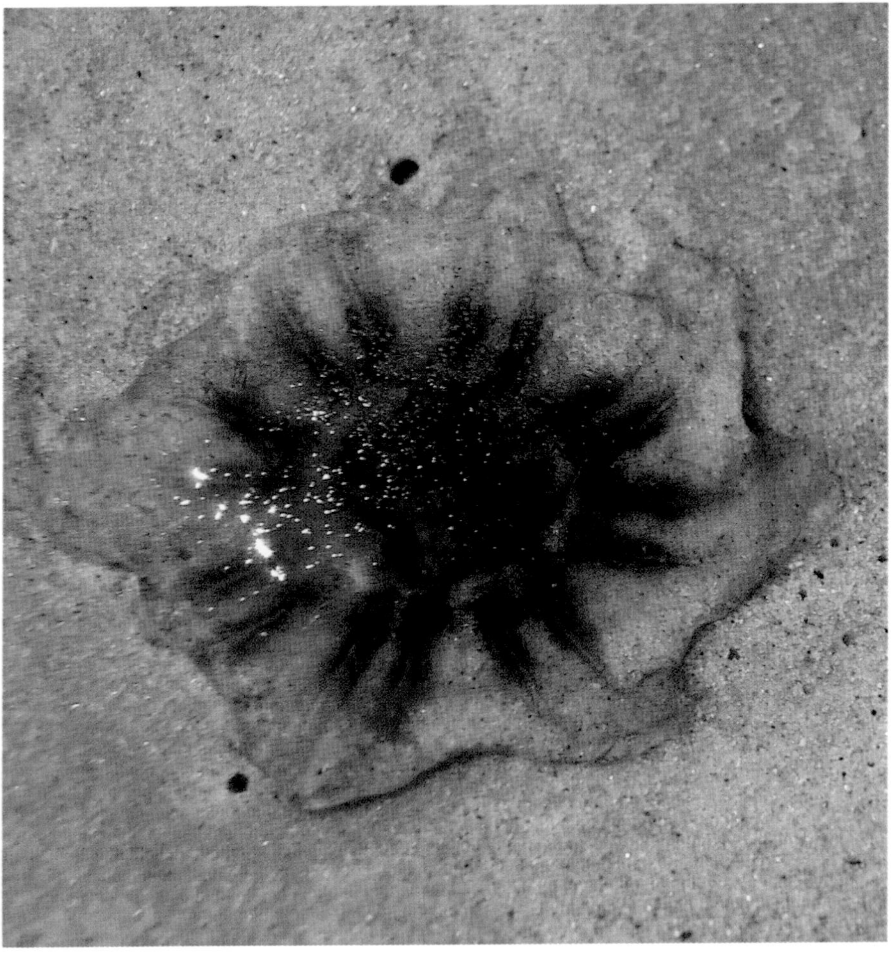

I saw a jellyfish.

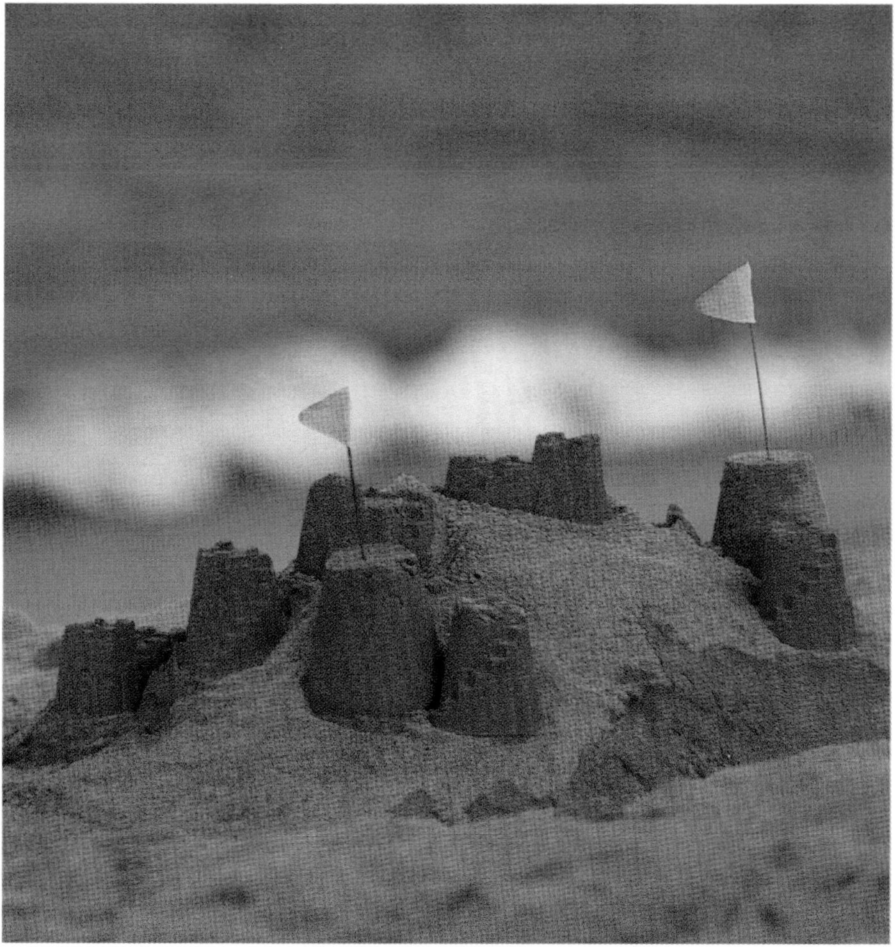

I saw a sand castle.

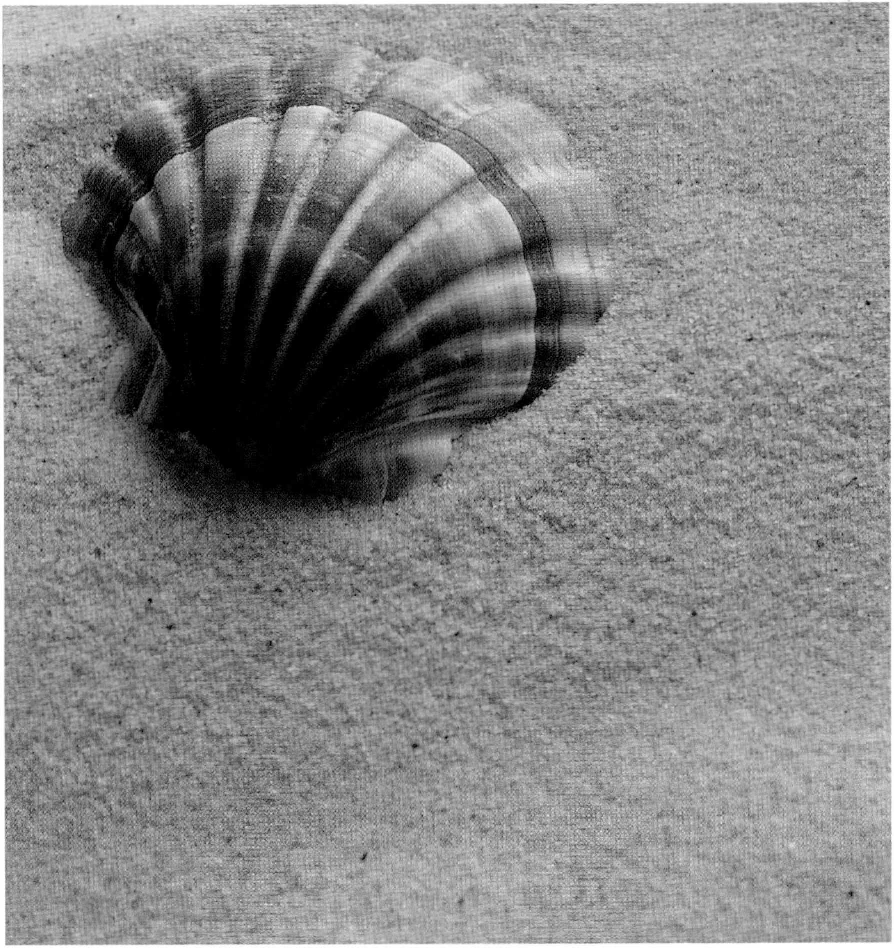

I saw a shell.

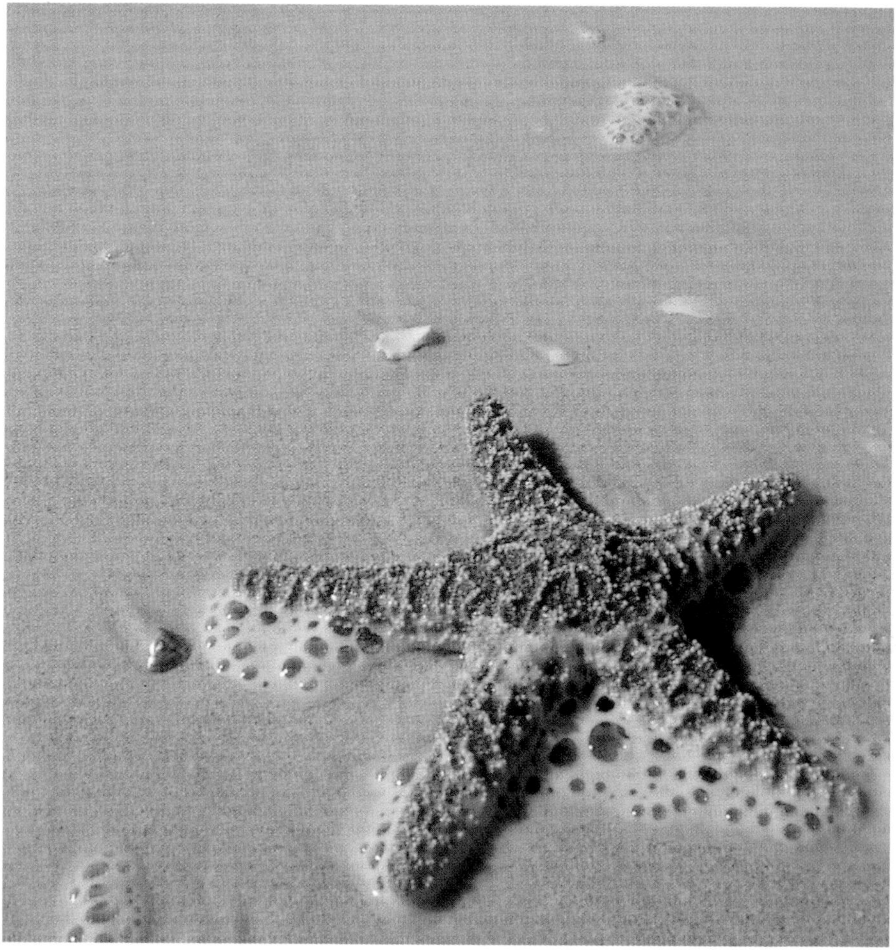

I saw a sea star.

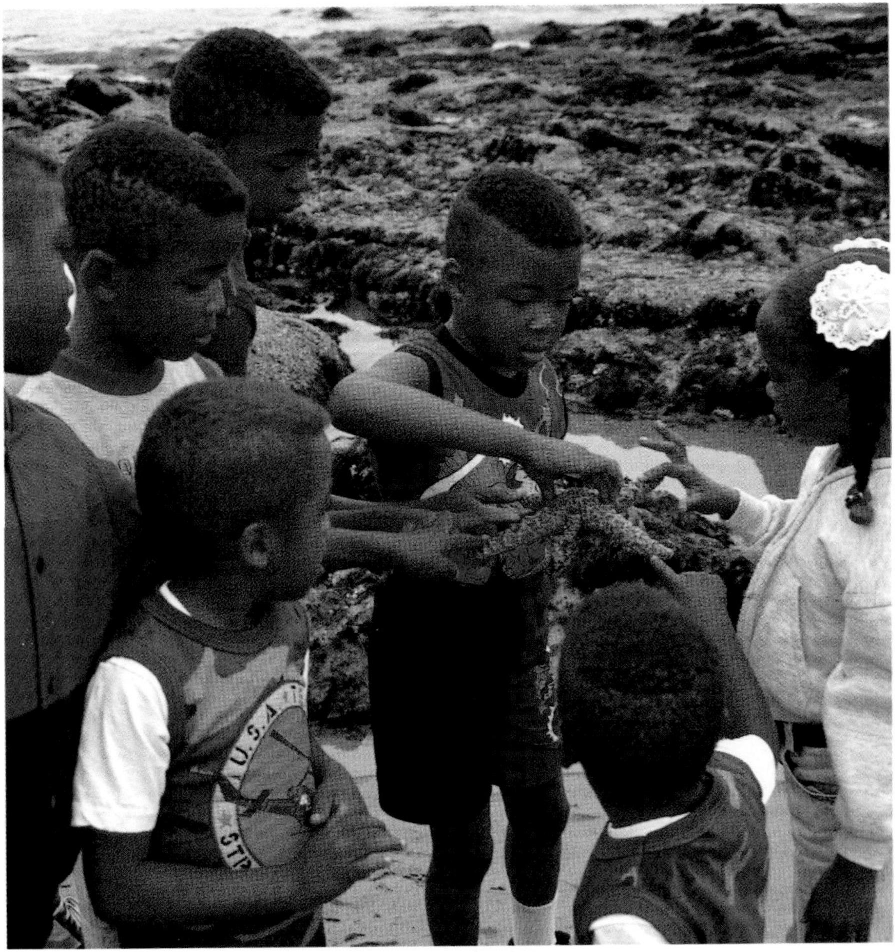

I picked it up.